THAT'S NOT A TOYKEY

BY JOE PATRINA AND JESSICA NOLAN

LittleHouse
WELCOME TO THE BARN

A CHILDREN'S LEARNING BOOK

JOE PATRINA AND JESSICA NOLAN– SINGERS IN THE BAND LITTLEHOUSE – COLLABORATED ON THIS BOOK WHEN JOE CALLED A PELICAN A TOYKEY AND LITTLE JAYLEE ROSE SAID "THATS'S NOT TOYKEY, THAT'S A SEAGULL."

FOR MORE ON LITTLEHOUSE GO TO

LITTLEHOUSELIVE.COM

Look Jaylee it's a Toykey

That's not a Toykey!
That's a Robin

and it goes
"Tweet Tweet"

Hey Jaylee that's a
Toykey!

Nope, this is a
Parrot and it says
"Hello"

Look down there Jaylee,
it's a Toykey!

No that's a Crow
and it goes "Caw Caw"

Look Jaylee a Toykey!

That's **not** a Toykey!

That's a Penguin and it says
"Twa Twa"

Look a Toykey!

That's no Toykey its an Ostrich and it says "Hiss Hiss"

Look up Jaylee it's a Toykey!

That's an old
Buzzard and it goes
"Heeee"

Look next to you Jaylee it's a Toykey!

That's no Toykey, this is a Duck

"Quack Quack"

Hey Jaylee it's a Toykey!

Awww, no it's a cute baby chick.

"Peep Peep"

Jaylee, look at that Toykey

Woah that's not a Toykey...

that's a Bald Eagle.

It says

"Ki Ki"

Look Jaylee
a Toykey!

A Toykey? NOOOO

That's a silly Goose!

"Honk Honk"

Shhhhh... look it's a Toykey

Wrong again, that's a Hummingbird

"Hummmmmmmm"

Look, over there a Toykey!

No thats a Bluebird

It says
"Tot Tu Tu"

Look Jaylee, finally a Toykey!!

That's NOT a Toykey!!!
That's a Sea Gull

it goes "Ha Ha Ha"

Look Jaylee it's a
Toykey, Toykey, Toykey!

That's not a Toykey, Toykey, Toykey

It's a
Turkey!
Turkey!
TURKEY!

"Gobble Gobble"